# Sun, Sand
## and
# Sausage Pie

# Sun, Sand and Sausage Pie

...and Beach House Memories

A cookbook by Sally Holbrook

SABILL PRESS
PASADENA, CALIFORNIA

Grateful acknowledgement is made to Amherst College, the Pasadena City Library and the Chi Phi Fraternity for their invaluable research assistance which has allowed the publisher to conclude that the poem "This Old House" by James S. Hamilton, which is reprinted in chapter 9, is now in the public domain.

Edited by Diane Macfarland
Design and art by Lauren Granito Designs
Printed by Henley Kutt & Associates

Publisher's Cataloging in Publication Data:
Holbrook, Sally
Sun, sand & sausage pie ... and beach
house memories: a cookbook
/by Sally Holbrook
p.cm
Includes index
1. Cookery, American.   I. title
TX 715      641.56

Library of Congress Catalog Card Number 91-91372
ISBN 0-9631225-0-9

SABILL PRESS
1440 Vista Lane
Pasadena, California 91103-1938

*This book is dedicated to my son, Billy. Without his encouragement and confidence in me, this book would never have been written. He died before it was finished, but his loving, gentle spirit guided me through each and every page.*

*And generous thanks to my nephew, Mike Boone, who helped me bring it all together.*

*Also, my gratitude to my husband, Bill, and to my friends Diane Macfarland and David Chaparro for their invaluable help and support.*

# Contents

# To Begin...

Many of us have fond memories of growing up in households where the kitchen was the center of activity. At the beach, ours was a large, sunny kitchen with a work table in the center. It was a wonderful place where my mother and grandmother spent hours lovingly preparing delicious meals, from simple fare to delectable party dishes, filling the house with mouth watering aromas.

When Mother died, she left behind a culinary legacy in the form of a large, carefully indexed, cloth bound book, which I found tucked inside a kitchen drawer. In it was a treasure house of recipes which she and my grandmother had used so often throughout the years.

Browsing through the book, I found recipes which brought back memories of times long forgotten. As I turned the pages, the joy and enthusiasm that had blessed each dish came flooding back to me. I want to share with you those recipes and the special memories which they inspired.

I hope this book will allow you to relive your own special memories of families gathered together to enjoy good times and great food.

# I Remember

Memories of the beach house are vivid and clear. I remember lazy days with family and friends; learning to swim while Daddy held me by a towel wrapped around my waist; sand in between my toes and sand in the sandwiches; appetites made ravenous by the sea air; a tranquil atmosphere created by a bayside view; June bugs, like dive bombers, invading our calm; fish on Friday, barbecues on Saturday, both teamed with fresh corn purchased from a nearby roadside stand; bread and rolls rising while, nearby, plump golden doughnuts popped to the top of bubbling oil.

On Fridays, we drove down from town after school was out, packed like sardines in the family roadster with running boards, and laden with enough clothes to last a year. Passing through miles of countryside dotted with dairy farms, my twin sister, Nancy, and I took turns reading the roadside Burma Shave signs. But the greatest fun was guessing who would be the first to see the water, for it was then that we knew we had arrived at the beach, and our house on the island.

During the summer months, Mother left Daddy behind in town while we stayed at the beach — but he joined us every weekend. The lids of large underground garbage boxes built into the curbside at the back of the house provided Nancy and me perfect seats on which to await his arrival. He called us "Snicklefritz" and "Snoodlepie," and brought us Sees chocolate lollipops. We helped him unload and, before you knew it, he was in bathing trunks and ready for a swim. Mother never swam with us because, she said, she always ended up swimming backwards. With the heat from the town washed away by a refreshing swim, Daddy was ready to enjoy a leisurely weekend.

My parents and grandparents often entertained their friends for lunch on the large brick patio overlooking the bay. A long collapsible wooden table was set up and spread with a blue and white checkered cloth. Hungry guests were often served a hearty Sausage Pie topped off with fresh summer fruit and homemade cookies for dessert. As the years progressed, my brother, sister and I added our own guests to the list of weekend visitors.

*Family, friends and Sausage Pie*
*Summer, 1937*

# Sausage Pie

1 cup white rice, uncooked
1 package frozen corn, thawed
1/2 green pepper, diced
1/2 red pepper, diced
1 tablespoon vegetable oil
4 to 5 medium tomatoes, peeled and diced
1 cup (about 4 ounces) sharp cheddar cheese, diced
1 tablespoon Worcestershire sauce
about 1 cup buttered bread crumbs
Jones link sausages, 3 to 4 per person

Cook rice according to package directions. Sauté peppers in oil about 3 minutes. Add to rice along with corn, tomatoes, cheese and Worcestershire sauce. Mix well. Place in shallow casserole. Top with buttered bread crumbs. Bake sausages on rack (in pan) in oven until lightly browned. Place on top of casserole. Bake in 350° oven for about 30 to 40 minutes. Serves 6 to 8.

# Elizabeth's French Bread

1/2 cup butter, softened
1/4 teaspoon paprika
1/4 teaspoon celery seed
1 loaf French bread, sliced

Spread bread slices with mixture of butter, paprika and celery seed. Re-form to tight loaf. Brush top lightly with same mixture. Wrap in foil. Heat in 375° oven for 20 minutes. Open foil to expose top of bread for the last 5 minutes in oven. Serves about 6 to 8.

# Green Salad Combinations

Using mixed greens, add a combination of sliced avocado, chunks of oranges or apples, sliced green or red onion, and slivered almonds. Toss with your favorite French dressing.

-- or --

Using mixed greens, add a combination of sliced avocado, cherry tomatoes, bacon pieces, sliced green onion, toasted pine nuts, walnuts or sunflower seeds, small chunks of Monterey Jack or Brie cheese and grated Parmesan cheese. Toss with your favorite dressing.

# Garlic Cream Dressing

1 large clove garlic, minced
1 teaspoon salt
1 cup salad oil
1/4 cup cider vinegar
1/4 cup heavy cream
1/2 cup sour cream

Beat together until well blended.

*I have found that adding slices of pimiento-stuffed green olives makes a delicious addition to this dressing.*

# French Dressing

1/4 cup red wine vinegar
3/4 cup salad oil
1/2 teaspoon Beau Monde
1/2 teaspoon *fines herbs*
1/2 teaspoon curry powder
1 teaspoon seasoning salt

Mix together in glass jar and shake well.

# Molasses Crumbles

3/4 cup (1 1/2 sticks) butter or margarine, softened
1 cup brown sugar, firmly packed
1 egg, beaten
4 tablespoons molasses
1/4 teaspoon salt
1/2 teaspoon cloves
1 teaspoon cinnamon
1 teaspoon ginger
2 1/2 cups flour
2 teaspoons baking soda
sugar for dipping

Cream butter and brown sugar. Blend in beaten egg and molasses. Sift dry ingredients. Add to above and mix well. Refrigerate for at least one hour. Roll into walnut size balls. Dip tops in sugar. Place on greased cookie sheet. Sprinkle each with a few drops of water. Bake in 350° oven for 12 minutes. Makes about 3 dozen.

# Oatmeal Cookies
# with Raisins or Chocolate Chips

1 1/2 cups sifted flour
1 teaspoon salt
3/4 cup brown sugar, firmly packed
3/4 cup sugar
1 cup shortening (butter or Crisco)
2 eggs, unbeaten
l teaspoon hot water
1 teaspoon baking soda
2 cups raisins or chocolate chips
2 cups rolled oats (oatmeal)
l cup chopped nuts
1 teaspoon vanilla

Sift flour and salt. Cream shortening and sugars. Add eggs, one at a time, beating after each and add to cream mixture. Dissolve soda in hot water and add to creamed mixture alternately with dry ingredients. Add nuts, raisins or chips, vanilla and oats. Drop by teaspoons onto greased cookie sheets. Bake in 350° oven for 12 to 15 minutes. Makes about 7 dozen.

*Using butter rather than Crisco makes these cookies a little richer; however, using Crisco will make them crispier.*

# Iced Chocolate Cookies

1 cup brown sugar, firmly packed
1/2 cup butter or Crisco
1 egg, unbeaten
1 1/2 cups flour
1/2 teaspoon baking powder
1/4 teaspoon salt
1/2 cup milk
2 squares (2 ounces) unsweetened chocolate, melted
3/4 cup chopped nuts
1 teaspoon vanilla

Cream brown sugar with butter or Crisco. Add egg and beat well. Add dry ingredients alternately with milk. Add chocolate, nuts and vanilla. Drop by teaspoons onto greased cookie sheet. Bake in 350° oven for 8 to 10 minutes. Cool and ice with icing below. Makes about 5 dozen cookies.

### Icing

2 squares (2 ounces) unsweetened chocolate, melted
1/3 cup butter or margarine
1 egg, unbeaten, room temperature
2 cups powdered sugar
1/4 teaspoon salt

Melt butter with chocolate over low heat. Cool slightly. Add remaining ingredients and beat until fluffy.

# Sour Cream Cookies

1/2 cup butter or Crisco
1 cup sugar
1 egg, unbeaten
2 cups flour
1/2 teaspoon baking powder
1/2 teaspoon baking soda
1/2 teaspoon salt
1/2 cup sour cream
juice and rind of 1/2 orange

Cream butter or Crisco with sugar. Add egg and beat well. Sift dry ingredients and add to above. Add sour cream with orange juice and rind. Drop by teaspoons onto greased cookie sheet. Bake in 375° oven for about 12 minutes. Cool and ice with icing below. Makes about 5 dozen.

### Icing

juice and rind of 1 lemon
powdered sugar

Mix juice and rind of lemon with powdered sugar to spreadable consistency.

*These have a delicate flavor and texture, and are my brother John's favorite.*

# Frosted Brownies

2 squares (2 ounces) unsweetened chocolate
1/3 cup shortening (butter or Crisco)
1 cup sugar
2 eggs, unbeaten
3/4 cup flour
1/2 teaspoon baking powder
1/2 teaspoon salt
1/2 cup nutmeats

Melt chocolate and shortening over boiling water. Beat in sugar and eggs. Sift together flour, baking powder and salt, and stir into above mixture. Spread in greased 8" square pan and bake in 350° oven for 30 minutes. Frost with frosting below. Makes about one dozen.

## Frosting

1 square (1 ounce) unsweetened chocolate
1 tablespoon butter
1 1/2 tablespoons hot water
1 cup powdered sugar

Melt chocolate and butter over boiling water. Blend in hot water. Stir in powdered sugar. Beat.

*When, as a young teenager, my son Bobby taught himself to cook, this was the first recipe he tried.*

*Later, just for fun, he added chocolate chips or mint flavored chocolate chips. Try it — it's different, and it's good.*

# Fish and Fame

We were fortunate to have a neighbor who was an avid fisherman. "Uncle Van Clothier" often supplied us with fresh albacore. When there was an overly abundant catch, he took it to the local cannery at the end of the island where it was packed in small cans for us to enjoy later.

We were forever fascinated with Uncle Van's stories of his childhood days growing up in the northern California mining town of Copperopolis. He treated himself to a martini or three on the weekends and, when anyone commented on his having more than one, he would answer, "when you have a martini, it makes a new man out of you — and then that new man wants a martini."

Another sportfishing neighbor, Leon Schlesinger, would occasionally surprise us with fresh swordfish. Mr. Schlesinger was the producer of the famous cartoon series Looney Tunes and Merry Melodies, and he often entertained celebrities on weekends. It was not unusual to see June Allyson and Dick Powell dropping by.

We were surrounded by Hollywood stars and producers. I shared family tales with Ann Southern, who rented the house next door one summer. Danny Milland, the handsome son of actor Ray Milland, frequently borrowed our funny old kayak. On some evenings we would walk down a few blocks to Jimmy Hixon's, the arranger for song writer Hoagy Carmichael, where we gathered around his piano and listened to him play "Stardust" and "Old Buttermilk Sky." Lana Turner, Rock Hudson and John Wayne also lived nearby.

As giggling, boy crazy teenagers, we rowed to the end of the island where Errol Flynn's boat, Sirocco, was anchored. We flirted with the crew and they threw us bottles of creme soda which we took home to be shared at cocktail time.

Meanwhile, all that glorious fish was being prepared for dinner! We broiled it with melted butter or baked it topped with sour cream and sliced almonds; we served it with baked potatoes, tomatoes, and creamy cucumbers. The grand finale was, as usual, one of the family's favorite desserts – Peach Pie or Western Pie.

*"Uncle Van Clothier" and Daddy with Albacore*
*Summer, 1946*

# Swordfish and Albacore

3 1/2 pounds of fillets will serve about 7 people with a small piece or two left for making Fish Salad. Baste the fillets with melted butter and broil on both sides until brown and flaky when pierced with a fork.

You can also bake the fish. Spread the fillets with a thick layer of sour cream and sprinkle slivered almonds over all. Bake in a 350° oven for 20 to 30 minutes, depending on thickness of fillets. They are done when they are flaky and the flesh is no longer translucent.

Serve the fish with baked potatoes, fresh summer corn, tomatoes and Cucumbers in Sour Cream, (see page 28).

 *To remove fish odors from your hands, rub them with slices of lemon.*

# Fish Salad

Cut leftover fish into chunks. Mix with a combination of mayonnaise, a spoonful of sour cream, chopped hard-boiled egg, sliced celery and sliced green onion. If there is any Tartar Sauce (see page 24) left you can either substitute it for the mayonnaise or mix half the mayonnaise and half the Tartar Sauce together.

# Tartar Sauce

Mix mayonnaise together with a small amount of sour cream. Add to that sweet pickle relish, dill (fresh or dry) and finely chopped green onion.

*Add a spoonful of Grandmother's Tangy Oil Pickles (see page 38) for an extra treat.*

*This Tartar Sauce is also delicious on baked potatoes served with the fish.*

# Curried Fried Tomatoes

4 to 6 unpeeled, firm, ripe tomatoes
salt, pepper
1/2 cup all purpose flour
1 teaspoon salt
3 tablespoons butter
1 teaspoon curry powder
milk or cream

Cut tomatoes into 1/2" slices, making about 12 slices in all. Sprinkle each with salt and pepper. Combine flour and salt. Dip slices into mixture, coating each side well. Heat butter in large skillet and stir in curry. Add tomatoes and brown on each side. Remove tomatoes and add enough milk or cream to make a sauce. Pour over tomatoes. Serves 6.

# Baked Curried Tomatoes

6 tomatoes
1 tablespoon curry powder
6 tablespoons butter
1 tablespoon sugar
1/2 teaspoon salt
chopped parsley

Cut tomatoes in half. Place cut side up in buttered casserole. Cream butter with curry, sugar, salt and pepper. Spread over tomatoes. Bake in 350° oven for 40 minutes. Sprinkle lightly with chopped parsley. Serves 8 to 10.

# Baked Whole Tomatoes

Cut a slice off the top of tomatoes and scoop out center pulp. Stuff with creamed spinach. Cover with buttered bread crumbs. Bake in 350° oven for 40 minutes. Sprinkle with chopped, crisply cooked bacon.

# Baked Tomato Halves

4 tablespoons chopped almonds
2 stalks celery, chopped
1/2 green pepper, chopped
1 bunch green onions, chopped
4 tomatoes, halved
2 tablespoons butter, melted

Place tomatoes in baking dish. Mix butter with rest of ingredients and spoon on top of tomato halves. Bake in 350° oven for about 20 minutes, or broil until bubbly.

# Baked Cheese Tomatoes

6 tomatoes, scalded and skinned
4 tablespoons butter
1/2 cup finely minced onion
3 tablespoons flour
3/4 cup light cream or milk
1 teaspoon salt
1/4 teaspoon pepper
1/8 teaspoon dry mustard
1/8 teaspoon nutmeg
dash of Worcestershire sauce
1/4 teaspoon basil
1 cup grated cheddar cheese
3/4 cup soft bread crumbs
1 cup soft, buttered bread crumbs (for topping)
salt and pepper

Cut a slice off tops of tomatoes and scoop out center pulp. Turn upside down and drain. Meanwhile, melt butter and add onion. Sauté onion until it is transparent, not brown. Blend in flour. Gradually add cream or milk, salt, pepper, mustard, nutmeg, Worcestershire and basil. Cook until thickened. Add cheese and 3/4 cup bread crumbs. Arrange tomatoes in shallow baking dish. Sprinkle inside with salt and pepper. Fill with mixture. Sprinkle top with 1 cup buttered bread crumbs. Bake in 375° oven for 15 to 20 minutes. Serves 4 to 6.

# Herbed Scalloped Tomatoes

4 cups canned tomatoes
1 1/2 cups Pepperidge Farm cubed herb seasoned stuffing
1 small onion, finely chopped
2 tablespoons sugar
1/2 teaspoon salt
1/2 teaspoon nutmeg
1/2 teaspoon oregano
1/4 teaspoon pepper
1/4 teaspoon rosemary
1 cup Pepperidge Farm cubed herb seasoned stuffing (for croutons)
2 tablespoons butter

Mix together first nine ingredients. Place in casserole dish. Dot with butter. Bake in 350° oven for 45 minutes. Meanwhile, sauté one cup stuffing in 2 tablespoons butter until lightly brown. Drain on paper towels. Serve as croutons and pass at the table. Serves 4 to 6.

*Leon Schlesinger with his skipper*
*Summer, 1941*

# Creamy Fried Tomatoes

6 large tomatoes
1 tablespoon flour
3/4 teaspoon salt
1/8 teaspoon pepper
1/4 cup margarine or butter
2 tablespoons flour
1 1/2 cups milk or cream
3/4 teaspoon salt
1 1/2 teaspoons sugar
1 1/2 teaspoons prepared mustard

Stem and halve tomatoes. Combine 1 tablespoon flour, salt and pepper. Sprinkle over tomatoes. Melt butter in skillet and sauté tomatoes on each side until just tender. Put 10 halves on heated serving platter. For the sauce, break up remaining two halves left in skillet, stir in 2 tablespoons flour, milk or cream and rest of ingredients. Cook until creamy. Pour over tomato halves. Serves 6 to 8.

# Cucumbers in Sour Cream

3 cucumbers, peeled and thinly sliced
1 cup sour cream
1 1/4 teaspoons salt
1/2 teaspoon dried dill
1/4 cup slivered or sliced almonds, toasted
3 tablespoons finely chopped chives
1/8 teaspoon pepper
1 tablespoon cider vinegar
1 teaspoon sugar

Mix all but the cucumbers, saving a few almonds for the top. Add cucumbers and place in serving bowl. Sprinkle remaining few almonds on top and chill. Serves 6.

# Peach Pie

4 tablespoons (1/2 stick) butter
1 cup sugar
2/3 cup flour
8 peaches, peeled and sliced
1 8" to 9" unbaked pie shell

Cream butter with sugar. Add flour and mix until "crumbly." Place half of mixture on bottom of pie shell. Mound peaches on top. Sprinkle other half of mixture evenly over peaches. Bake in 375° oven until bubbly and pie crust is brown, about 45 minutes. The "crumbly" mixture should form a crust of its own.

*It is easier to peel peaches if you drop them in boiling water for 40 to 60 seconds.*

*Brush bottom of the unbaked pie shell lightly with the white of an egg, or heavy cream, to keep it from becoming soggy.*

# Western Pie

1 1/2 cups cooked prunes, pitted and cut in half
1 1/2 cups sliced bananas
1/2 cup sugar
2 tablespoons cornstarch
2/3 cup prune juice
1/3 cup orange juice
2 tablespoons lemon juice
1 tablespoon butter
1/8 teaspoon salt
grated sharp cheddar cheese
1 8" baked pie shell

Place prunes in bottom of baked pie shell. Cover with bananas. Mix sugar and cornstarch. Moisten with a little prune juice to make a paste. Add rest of ingredients, except grated cheese, and cook until thick. Cool. Pour over prunes and bananas. Cover with grated cheese. Refrigerate.

Trust me, you'll love this!

*Weekend guests - March, 1934*

# Blazing Barbecues

As so well expressed in Lee Bailey's cookbook COUNTRY WEEKENDS, our weekend barbecues were "easy, relaxed and uncomplicated." After a leisurely afternoon sail and an invigorating swim, our appetites were enormous. Our Cocker Spaniel, with his swim behind him, also would be waiting for a tasty morsel to be tossed his way. Thirsty family and friends gathered for cocktails on the patio and raised their glasses to the parade of boaters passing by. Occasionally, a sailboat would snag a falling kite on its tall mast like a large butterfly caught in a net.

Hungry whining seagulls circled overhead and, at the most appropriate time, our favorite bay seal would surface and heave his shiny, black body onto the dock — his huge, round eyes watching us as we watched our barbecue fire turn to hot, dusty coals.

We used lighter fluid to start the charcoal, but only once did we have a close call. When the lighted match was tossed on the saturated coals, a huge wall of flames exploded upward and headed perilously close to a large, overhanging tree. It appeared to onlookers across the bay that we had a raging house fire in the making and, within minutes, two fireboats converged near the bulkhead, a helicopter began circling overhead and two fire trucks appeared at the street end. We were quickly surrounded by a crowd of curious neighbors. As the fire settled down, the emergency crews departed and the crowd quietly dispersed. Although we were a bit chagrined, the barbecue preparations continued uninterrupted!

We marinated steaks, chuck roasts and shish kebobs. Chicken and spareribs were bathed in tangy sauces accompanied with potatoes or rice. For dessert, we somehow managed to find room for Graham Cracker Pie or Jumbles and ice cream which had been enthusiastically hand cranked in an antique freezer by the younger family members.

To accompany the beef, we heaped generous portions of Grandmother's Tangy Oil Pickles onto our plates, proud that we had all helped in slicing the tiny cucumbers while sitting on the porch on a sunny summer day.

*John supervising Daddy at the Barbecue*
*Weekend 1936*

## Marinade for Lamb Shish Kebob

3 1/2 to 4 pounds of lamb, cut into 1 1/2" cubes
grated rind of 1/2 lemon
2 cloves garlic, crushed
3 large onions, chopped
1/2 teaspoon pepper
1 tablespoon dry mustard
1 tablespoon dried oregano
1 tablespoon salt
juice of four lemons

Place all ingredients in plastic bag (for easy turning); place bag in bowl and refrigerate. Let stand several hours or overnight, turning occasionally.

## Marinade for Lamb Shanks

1 clove garlic, crushed
1 cup diced onion
2 tablespoons olive oil
1 1/2 cups chopped tomatoes
1 cup diced green pepper
1 cup diced celery
1/2 cup catsup
2 tablespoons brown sugar
1 teaspoon dry mustard
2 cups lamb or beef stock or broth
1 teaspoon salt
1 teaspoon chili powder
1 teaspoon Worcestershire sauce
2 slices lemon
6 lamb shanks

Sauté onion and garlic in oil. Add other ingredients and place in plastic bag, place bag in bowl and refrigerate for several hours or overnight, turning occasionally. Shanks may be precooked in oven and then basted with marinade on barbecue.

## Quick and Easy Marinade for Spareribs

Using 1 pound of ribs per person, place in roasting pan and cook, uncovered, in 350° oven for 1 hour. Pour off grease and barbecue or bake another half hour. Baste with a sauce consisting of equal amounts of catsup and A-1 Steak Sauce. Thin with a little water.

## Marinade for Sirloin Steak or Chuck Roast

1/2 cup soy sauce
1/2 cup lemon juice
1/2 cup olive oil
1 bay leaf
1/2 teaspoon seasoned pepper
1 6 pound roast or 2 large steaks

Place all ingredients in a plastic bag, place in bowl. Refrigerate for at least 24 hours, turning occasionally.

*Marinades can be prepared several days in advance if kept in the refrigerator.*

# Marinade for Steaks, Roasts, Beef Shish Kebob

2 cloves garlic, finely minced
2 tablespoons olive oil
1/4 teaspoon dry mustard
1 teaspoon soy sauce
1/2 teaspoon dried rosemary
2 tablespoons red wine vinegar
4 tablespoons burgundy wine
2 tablespoons catsup
1/2 teaspoon Worcestershire sauce
1 1/2 teaspoons A-1 Steak Sauce

Sauté garlic in oil. Add mustard, soy sauce and rosemary. Remove from heat and stir in wine vinegar and wine. Pour over meat and marinate for 24 hours, turning occasionally. Prior to barbecuing, remove meat from marinade. Add to the marinade catsup, Worcestershire sauce and A-1 Steak Sauce. Apply some to the meat and baste with the rest.

*When the barbecue coals are red hot, toss in a few cloves of garlic directly under the meat.*

## Marinade for Chicken and/or Spareribs

1 cup Chris and Pitts barbecue sauce
1 cup catsup
1/4 cup soy sauce
3 tablespoons Worcestershire sauce
2 cloves garlic, crushed
1/4 cup red wine vinegar
1/3 cup brown sugar, firmly packed
1/4 cup bourbon
1/4 cup Dijon mustard

Bake chicken and/or ribs in 350° oven for 1 hour.  Mix the above ingredients.  Place chicken pieces and/or ribs in large pan and cover with sauce.  Refrigerate and let stand overnight.  Barbecue and baste with residual marinade.

## New Potatoes in Herb Sauce

1/4 cup butter
1 tablespoon olive oil
juice and peel from 1/2 small lemon
1 tablespoon minced green onion
1 tablespoon dried thyme
1 tablespoon chopped parsley
4 new potatoes, peeled and cooked

Melt butter in small sauce pan and add together first six ingredients.  Pour over hot potatoes.  Serves 4.

# Mashed Potato "Popovers"

*For each cup of cooled mashed potatoes add:*
1 egg, beaten
1 tablespoon melted butter
1 tablespoon milk or cream
1 teaspoon baking powder
2 tablespoons flour
pinch of salt

Mix thoroughly. Bake in greased muffin tins in 375° oven until browned and thoroughly heated, about 35 to 40 minutes.
Serves 4 to 6.

*These are particularly good with spareribs.*
*Also, this is a nice way of serving leftover mashed potatoes.*

# Potatoes Alice

3 large baking potatoes
3 eggs, unbeaten
2 cups half and half
1 heaping cup grated Swiss cheese
salt and pepper

Slice potatoes very thin and arrange in layers with Swiss cheese. Beat eggs and half and half. Pour over potato and cheese mixture. Bake in 325° oven, uncovered, for 1 hour. Serves 4 to 6.

# Hot Gingered Papaya

2 firm, ripe papayas, cut in half lengthwise
4 tablespoons butter
2 tablespoons lime juice
1/4 teaspoon ground ginger
dash of cayenne pepper

Remove seeds from papayas. Arrange in greased casserole. Melt butter, add lime juice and ginger. Spoon into cavity of each papaya. Bake in 350° oven for 30 minutes, basting often. Serve hot with a dash of cayenne pepper. Serves 4.

# Grandmother's Tangy Oil Pickles

25 small pickling cucumbers
1 tablespoon celery seed
1 cup mustard seed
1/2 cup non-iodized salt
1 quart white vinegar
1/2 cup olive oil

Slice cucumbers very thin, do not peel. Put into gallon size stone crock with loose fitting lid. Mix rest of ingredients and pour over cucumbers. Stir at least once a day for several days to one week. Should not be refrigerated or oil will gel. Makes about 2 quarts.

*My nephew, Mike, eats these by the dishful. They are delicious on hot dogs, with pot roast, and make a great addition to homemade Tartar Sauce.*

# Chili Sauce

4 quarts, or 8 pounds, tomatoes, peeled and diced
1/2 large bunch celery, chopped fine
1 pound white onions, peeled and chopped fine
1 green pepper, chopped fine
3 cups white vinegar
2 tablespoons salt

Combine ingredients and cook until reduced by half, about 2 hours, then add:

1 pound brown sugar
1/2 teaspoon cinnamon
1 small bottle prepared horseradish
1/2 teaspoon pepper
1/2 teaspoon powdered cloves

Cook until thick, about 1 hour.   Refrigerate — but not for more than one week!  This is a wonderful recipe for canning.  Makes about 4 quarts.

*My husband says to try this on barbecued hamburgers for a real treat!*

# Graham Cracker Pie

### Crust:

1 1/3 cups graham crackers, crushed fine
1/2 cup (1 stick) melted butter
1 teaspoon flour
1/2 cup sugar

Mix and pat half into 8" to 9" pie pan (saving half for topping).

### Filling:

3 egg yolks (save whites for topping)
1/2 cup sugar
2 cups milk
2 tablespoons cornstarch
1 teaspoon vanilla

Cook all ingredients in double boiler until thick. Pour into shell.

### Topping:

3 egg whites, beaten
3 tablespoons sugar

Beat egg whites until stiff. Fold in sugar. Spread on pie. Top with remaining half of crust. Bake in 350° oven for 20 to 25 minutes, until lightly browned.

# Jumbles

2 cups sugar
1 cup Crisco
1 cup sour cream
3 eggs, beaten
4 cups flour
1 heaping teaspoon each cinnamon, allspice and nutmeg
1 small rounded teaspoon baking soda
1 teaspoon salt
2 tablespoons sugar (for topping)
1 teaspoon cinnamon

Cream sugar and Crisco. Add sour cream and eggs. Sift together flour, spices, baking soda and salt. Add to above. Spoon into greased muffin cups and sprinkle with the mixture of cinnamon and sugar. Bake in 350° oven for 15 to 20 minutes, depending on size of muffin tins, and until cake tester comes out clean. Makes about 24 small and 10 large Jumbles.

# Peaches and Brandy

Skin peaches (see helpful note under Peach Pie, page 29), halve and remove pit, and place in shallow bake dish. In each half, place 1 teaspoon brandy, 1 heaping teaspoon brown sugar. Dot with butter. Bake in 350° oven for about 1/2 hour. Serve with ice cream or heavy cream and Jumbles (see above).

# Wintry Pleasures

By November, the weather had turned cold and we were forced to spend more time inside. When it rained, we had to share the only inside shower or venture outside to the swimmers' crude showers, often facing drenching rain and biting winds.

Meals were served at a large refectory table that had been polished to a golden sheen. Mother was a pro at providing us with a variety of hearty lunches. Surrounded by knotty pine walls and the glow of a warm fire, we watched brave boaters sailing by, securely wrapped in their yellow slickers, while we lunched on Broiled Club Sandwiches and Hot Bostons.

Mother's black bean soup was a quick warmer-upper. Piping hot soup was poured into individual bowls with a slice of lemon and one hard-boiled egg, sliced, in each bowl. Homemade rolls, breads and cookies completed the satisfying meal.

At dinner time we basked in a view enhanced by candlelight, as we watched the moon rise and spread its light over the darkening bay. The salty, fish-scented breeze sent the water lazily lapping up and down the smooth sand. After dinner we played Monopoly and Parcheesi, or we pulled down the World War II blackout curtains and watched family movies — with the film usually ending up in a tangled heap on the floor.

Our dinner menus included gourmet fare such as Fish Cooked in Wine; Chicken Paprika with Corn Pancakes; Curried Chicken, fish or beef served with a Fruited Rice Ring. And for dessert, Gingerbread with Foamy Sauce or tangy Lemon Pudding.

*Nancy and Sally at 16 months*
*Winter, 1933*

# Hot Bostons

6 slices white bread
1 large can baked beans, about 2 1/2 cups
1 cup thousand island dressing
1 tablespoon minced onion

Toast bread slices on one side. Mix beans, dressing, and onion. Mound on untoasted side of bread. Place under the broiler and heat until bubbly. Serves 4 to 6.

# Broiled Club Sandwiches

6 slices white bread
soft butter or mayonnaise
6 thin slices of ham and turkey
6 thin slices of tomato
6 slices of sharp cheddar cheese
6 slices of bacon, cut in half

Toast bread on one side and lightly moisten the other side with butter or mayonnaise. Place ingredients, in above order, on top of buttered side of bread. Broil until cheese melts and bacon is cooked. You may prefer to pre-fry the bacon, slightly, to insure its crispness. Serves 4 to 6.

# Grilled Corned Beef on Rye

Spread slices of rye or pumpernickel bread with thousand island dressing. Top with corned beef, sauerkraut, sliced tomatoes and sliced Swiss cheese. Cover with another slice of bread. Butter both sides of sandwich. Grill until hot and cheese has melted. Anchor with toothpick pinned through a stuffed green olive.

# Poppyseed Dressing for Fruit Salad

3/4 cups sugar
2 teaspoons salt
1/2 teaspoon dry mustard
2 tablespoons poppy seeds
1/4 teaspoon celery seeds
1 tablespoon grated onion
2/3 cup red wine vinegar
2 cups salad oil

Mix together sugar, salt, mustard, poppy seeds, celery seeds and grated onion. Stir in vinegar. With electric beater going, add the oil a little at a time until blended and thickened. Refrigerate. Pour over fresh fruit or a salad of avocado and grapefruit sections.

# Fresh Pear Salad

Mix 1 cup cottage cheese and 3 tablespoons each mayonnaise and orange or ginger marmalade. Place pear halves, peeled and cored, on lettuce lined plates and top with dressing. Sprinkle with a little nutmeg. Garnish each serving with a slice of orange.

# Banana Salad

Using one banana per person, split lengthwise and place on lettuce lined plate. Place a dollop of mayonnaise on each slice of banana and sprinkle generously with coarsely chopped peanuts.

*If you have any leftover whipped cream, you might want to fold a little into the mayonnaise for a lighter texture.*

# Orange Muffins

1/4 cup (1/2 stick) butter, softened
1/3 cup sugar
1 tablespoon grated orange rind
1 egg, beaten
1 1/2 cups cake flour (see page 78)
2 teaspoons baking powder
1 teaspoon salt
1/4 cup milk
1/4 cup orange juice, strained

Cream butter with the sugar and orange rind. Add egg and beat well. Sift together flour, baking powder and salt and add to the above, alternately, with milk mixed with the orange juice. Fill greased muffin tins and bake in 400° oven for about 15 to 20 minutes. Makes 6 large muffins.

# Lazy Day Rolls

2 packages yeast
1/3 cup sugar
1 cup milk, scalded and cooled to lukewarm
1/4 cup (1/2 stick) butter, melted
1 teaspoon grated orange rind
3 eggs, beaten
4 cups flour
1 teaspoon salt
additional melted butter
pecan halves
brown sugar

Let combined yeast and sugar stand 5 minutes. Add milk, 1/4 cup melted butter, orange rind, salt and eggs. Mix well. Add flour and beat slowly until mixed. Cover and let rise until double in bulk. Punch down. Into individually greased muffin cups, place 1 teaspoon melted butter, 1 pecan half and 1/2 teaspoon brown sugar. With flowered hands, pull off chunks of dough and make balls slightly larger than a golf ball and place in the muffin tin. Let rise until doubled. Bake in 350° oven for 15 to 20 minutes. Makes about 2 dozen.

*I call these "upside down" rolls because of the sweet surprise at the bottom.*

*These are particularly nice for breakfast with company.*

# Sunday Hot Bread

3/4 cup sugar
2 tablespoons soft butter
1 egg, well beaten
1/2 cup milk
1 teaspoon vanilla
1 1/2 cups flour
1/8 teaspoon salt
3 teaspoons baking powder
2 tablespoons sugar (for topping)
1 teaspoon cinnamon

Cream butter and sugar. Add egg. Mix with milk and vanilla. Sift flour, salt and baking powder and add to creamed mixture. Spread in buttered 9" pan and sprinkle liberally with the mixture of cinnamon and sugar. Bake in 400° oven for 15 minutes or until tester comes out clean.

*Houseparty, 1944*

# Baked Fish with Wine

2 pounds halibut fillets
1 large onion, sliced
1 cup white wine
3 tablespoons butter
2 medium tomatoes, sliced
1/2 green pepper, chopped
salt

Sprinkle fillets with salt. Cover with onion. Pour wine over all. Let soak 1/2 hour. Melt butter in shallow pan. Remove fish from onions and wine and place in a bake dish. Cover with tomatoes, green peppers and onions. Bake in 350° oven for about 35 minutes, basting occasionally with remaining wine marinade. Serves 4.

# Chicken Paprika

1 frying chicken (3 to 4 pounds), cut into serving pieces
2 tablespoons butter
2 tablespoons vegetable oil
5 tablespoons flour
2 cups water
1 cup sour cream
1 1/2 rounded teaspoons paprika
1/2 cup sauterne wine
salt and pepper

Dust chicken with salt and pepper. In large skillet, fry in butter and oil until brown on all sides. Remove from pan. Add flour to drippings and blend. Add water, sour cream, paprika and wine. Cook, stirring constantly, until thick and smooth. Return chicken to pan and cover. Simmer for one hour or until tender. Arrange chicken on platter. Season gravy with salt and pepper and pour over chicken. Serves 4.

# Nancy's Oyster Stuffed Chicken

2 broilers, split
6 1/2 ounce can of oysters
3 tablespoons chopped green pepper
2 tablespoons chopped celery
3 tablespoons chopped parsley
2 tablespoons chopped onion
1 clove garlic, crushed
4 tablespoons (1/2 stick) butter
1 cup coarse, fresh bread crumbs
1/4 teaspoon cayenne
1 teaspoon salt
1/4 teaspoon pepper
1/4 cup white wine
1/4 cup water
melted butter

Drain and chop oysters, saving liquid. Sauté oysters with seasonings and vegetables in 4 tablespoons of butter for 10 minutes; do not brown. Add bread crumbs and 1/2 cup oyster liquid, adding water if needed to bring it up to 1/2 cup. Place chicken skin side up in shallow bake dish and dot with butter. Add white wine and water to pan. Bake in 375° oven for 1 hour. Remove from oven. Turn skin side down and fill cavities with bread crumb mixture. Pour a little melted butter over all. Bake 30 minutes more, until golden brown. Serves 4.

# Veal with Almonds

1 1/2 pounds veal steak, sliced thin
1 to 2 tablespoons vegetable oil
1 small carton sour cream
2 beef bouillon cubes
1 cup hot water
sliced almonds, about 1/2 cup, browned in butter
salt, pepper
3/4 package noodles

Cut veal into serving size pieces. Season with salt and pepper and brown in oil in large frypan. Remove veal and add sour cream. Dissolve bouillon cubes in hot water and add to pan. Return veal to pan. Cover and cook over low heat 20 to 25 minutes, or until veal is tender. Cook noodles. Arrange on serving platter with veal on top. Pour over sauce from pan. Sprinkle with almonds. Serves 4.

# Southern Pork Chops

4 large sweet potatoes
3/4 cup brown sugar, firmly packed
2 oranges
6 thick pork chops
salt, pepper

Cook potatoes, skin and slice. Slice oranges. Layer potatoes and oranges in casserole and sprinkle with brown sugar. Brown chops. Season with salt and pepper and arrange on potatoes and oranges. Add about a cup of water to the pan in which chops have been browned, scraping up browned bits, and pour over chops. Cover, bake in 350° oven for 1 1/2 hours, basting frequently. Serves 4.

# Baked Steak

1 large top sirloin steak, 1" to 1 1/2" thick
- or -
individual fillet mignon steaks
tomato slices 1/2" thick
onion slices 1/4" thick
lemon slices 1/4" thick
bacon strips slightly precooked

Score top of steak, or steaks, and season both sides with salt and pepper.  Brush with margarine or butter and place in shallow pan. Cover with slices of tomatoes, onions, lemons, and strips of bacon.

Secure with toothpicks.  Sprinkle with a few drops of vegetable oil. Bake in 400° oven for 45 minutes for the top sirloin and about 25 minutes for the fillet mignon.  They will be medium rare.

*If the threat of rain prevents you from barbecuing, try baking your steak instead.  It's a real treat!*

# Pork Tenderloin with Prunes

For each tenderloin, "soak six handsome prunes in tepid water." When the prunes are "somewhat swollen" drain, pit and cook them slowly in a small quantity of water mixed equally with port or Madeira wine. Cut pork tenderloin, free of fat, into slices 1/2" thick. Season with salt and pepper. Dredge lightly with flour and brown slowly and thoroughly in butter on both sides. Arrange the meat in a ring on a heated serving platter and put the prunes in the center. Add 2 tablespoons brandy to the frying pan. *Using extreme caution,* set aflame and shake until all alcohol has burned out. Stir in 1/4 to 1/2 cup heavy cream. Simmer for a minute and pour over pork and prunes.

*The quaintness of the words reflect the language of the times when this recipe was written.*

# Fruited Rice Ring for Curries

4 cups cooked rice
1/2 cup orange marmalade
1/4 cup raisins
salt, pepper

Combine and pack firmly into well greased 1 quart ring mold. Set in pan of hot water and bake at 350° long enough to heat through, 35 to 45 minutes. Unmold and fill center with curried chicken, seafood, meat or eggs. Serves 4 to 6.

# Baked Acorn Squash with Apples

6 tart apples
1/2 cup brown sugar, firmly packed
2 tablespoons lemon juice
1/4 heaping teaspoon nutmeg
1/4 heaping teaspoon cinnamon
1/2 to 3/4 cup grated sharp cheddar cheese
4 medium acorn squash
8 teaspoons butter
additional grated sharp cheddar cheese

Wash, core, pare and dice apples. Add brown sugar, lemon juice, nutmeg, cinnamon and 1/2 to 3/4 cup of cheese. Wash squash and cut in half crosswise, removing seeds. Cut thin slice off bottoms so they will stand up. Fill centers with apple mixture. Top each half with a teaspoon of butter. Place in baking pan filled with 1" of water. Cover. Bake in 375° oven for 1 hour and 15 minutes. Remove cover and lightly sprinkle additional grated cheese over top. Bake 5 to 10 minutes longer. Serves 8.

# Eggplant Parmigiana

1 large eggplant
1 1/2 cups meatless spaghetti sauce
1/2 pound Mozzarella cheese, sliced
6 tablespoons grated Parmesan cheese
fine, dry bread crumbs

Peel eggplant. Slice into 1/2" slices and coat each one in breading mix. Brown in hot oil. Place in shallow casserole. Distribute sauce over eggplant, then cheeses, beginning with the Mozzarella. Broil until the cheese has melted. Serves 4.

# Zucchini Patties

5 medium zucchini
3 eggs, unbeaten
2 tablespoons flour
1 teaspoon salt
1 teaspoon pepper
1 tablespoon grated Parmesan cheese
1/2 cup finely chopped parsley
oil for frying

Wash zucchini. Remove ends and shred coarsely. Press out water. Mix with rest of ingredients except the oil. Heat a small amount of oil in fry pan. Shape zucchini into patties and sauté until lightly browned on each side. Add more oil as needed.

# Maple Butter Glazed Carrots

2 pounds carrots
1/4 cup maple syrup
1/4 cup (1/2 stick) butter or margarine
toasted, slivered almonds

Pare carrots. Slice diagonally into 1" slices. Cook in slightly salted water until just tender. Drain. Heat syrup and butter in skillet over low heat for 2 to 3 minutes or until slightly thickened. Add carrots and cook until glazed. Sprinkle with toasted almonds. Serves 4.

# Harvard Beets

1/2 cup sugar
1/2 tablespoon cornstarch
1/2 cup cider vinegar
1 large can or jar of whole beets
2 tablespoons butter

Mix sugar and cornstarch. Add vinegar. Let boil for 5 minutes. Add beets and let stand 1/2 hour. Add butter and reheat before serving. Serves 4.

# Cornmeal Pancakes

2 eggs, well beaten
1 1/2 cups milk, room temperature
1/3 cup butter, melted
salt
1 cup flour
2 1/2 teaspoons baking powder
1/2 cup yellow cornmeal
1/2 cup corn, fresh or frozen
vegetable oil

Mix egg, milk, butter and salt. Add flour and baking powder and mix until blended. Add cornmeal, then mix in corn. Brush skillet with oil and heat. Pour a small amount of batter into skillet. Fry until golden. Serve with melted butter. Makes about 18 medium pancakes.

# Lemon Pudding with Lemon Sauce

1 cup sugar
1 heaping tablespoon flour
1 cup milk, room temperature
3 egg yolks, beaten
juice of 2 lemons
rind of one lemon, grated
1 tablespoon butter, melted and cooled
pinch of salt
3 egg whites, beaten until stiff

Mix sugar and flour. Add milk. Mix egg yolks with lemon juice and rind. Add to sugar, flour and milk. Stir in butter and salt. Fold in beaten egg whites. Bake in buttered 1 quart ovenproof dish which has been set in a pan of hot water. Bake in 350° oven for 45 to 60 minutes until golden brown. Serve with Lemon Sauce, see below. Serves 4.

### Lemon Sauce

1/2 cup sugar
1 tablespoon cornstarch
1 cup boiling water
2 tablespoons butter
1 1/2 tablespoons lemon juice
few gratings fresh nutmeg

Mix sugar and cornstarch. Add water gradually, stirring constantly. Boil for 5 minutes. Remove from fire and add the rest of the ingredients.

*This sauce is also delicious over warm gingerbread.*

# Gingerbread with Foamy Sauce

1/2 cup (1 stick) butter
1/2 cup sugar
1 egg, beaten
1 cup molasses
2 1/2 cups flour
1 1/2 teaspoons baking soda
1 teaspoon cinnamon
1 teaspoon ginger
1/2 teaspoon powdered cloves
1/2 teaspoon salt
1 cup hot water

Cream butter and sugar. Add egg and molasses. Sift together flour, baking soda, cinnamon, ginger, cloves and salt. Add to creamed mixture. Add hot water and beat until smooth (batter will be thin). Bake in greased 9"x13" pan in 325° oven for 35 minutes, or until cake tester comes out clean. Makes about 12 medium size pieces. Serve with Foamy Sauce, see below.

### Foamy Sauce

3/4 cup powdered sugar
2 egg yolks
1/2 pint whipping cream
1 teaspoon vanilla

Cream sugar and egg yolks. Whip cream and add the vanilla. Fold egg mixture into the cream mixture. Serves 5. This recipe can easily be doubled.

# Party Pears

4 fresh pears, skinned, halved and cored
8 teaspoons cocoa
6 egg yolks
2/3 cup sugar
1 cup Marsala or white wine
1 tablespoon kirsch or rum

Prepare simple syrup (2 cups water and 1/2 cup sugar boiled for 3 minutes).  Poach pears in syrup until soft.  Lift pears from syrup and fill center cavity of each half with 1 teaspoon cocoa.  Fasten the two halves together with toothpicks and set aside.  Whip sugar and egg yolks together in top of a double boiler over low heat.  Add wine, slowly, stirring constantly.  When mixture starts to thicken, remove from heat and stir in kirsch or rum.  Chill for several hours.  Place pears on individual plates and cover with sauce.  Serves 4.

*Lido Isle, 1932*

# Easter

After school was out for the Easter holiday, we invited friends to join us at the beach for several carefree days of sun, sand and frivolity. We swam in the chilly water and smeared ourselves with iodine-laced baby oil with hopes of getting a glamorous tan to show off when we returned to school. By the end of the first day we looked more like freckled lobsters than bronzed bathing beauties.

When cooler weather sent us inside, we played card games, told fortunes and held séances. We worked seriously at "lifting the table," which scared us half to death when the table actually left the floor. We burst into near-hysterical giggles when the "ghost" of a neighbor looking for his dog appeared in the inner courtyard during one very intense moment.

By the time the weekend rolled around, only family members remained to prepare for Easter Day. Saturday we dyed and decorated eggs. After we had gone to bed, Mother hid them in and around the living room, finding some very creative places to conceal them. Sunday morning, with our Easter baskets in hand, we hunted for the eggs and colorfully wrapped packages containing stuffed animals, games and books. We concluded the morning festivities with a large breakfast of scrambled eggs, bacon and Hopi's Sugar Glazed Easter Bunny Rolls.

The eggs collected during the morning were sliced into black bean soup or made into deviled egg sandwiches in time for lunch. Dinner was the only formal meal of the week. Four generations gathered at the dinner table for a leg of lamb baked on a bed of thinly sliced potatoes and onions. We finished the meal with Auntie Coleman's White Cake with Broiled Icing.

*Sally and Nancy*
*Easter, 1936*

# Hopi's Sugar Glazed Easter Bunny Rolls

1 package dry yeast
1/4 cup warm water
1 cup milk, scalded
1/3 cup sugar
1/2 cup (1 stick) butter or Crisco
1 teaspoon salt
5 to 5 1/2 cups flour
2 eggs, beaten
1/4 cup orange juice
2 tablespoons grated orange peel

Soften yeast in warm water. Combine scalded milk, sugar, butter or Crisco and salt. Cool until lukewarm; stir in about 2 cups of flour. Add eggs and mix well. Stir in softened yeast. Add orange juice and peel and enough of the remainder of flour to make a soft dough. Cover; let rest 10 minutes. Knead 5 to 10 minutes on lightly floured surface until smooth and elastic. Place in lightly greased bowl, turning once to grease surface. Cover; let rise in warm place until double. Punch down, cover, and let rise 10 minutes. Shape (see instructions on page 64), cover and let rise in warm place until light and nearly double in size. Bake in 375° oven 12 to 15 minutes. Frost while warm with Sugar Glaze. Makes about 2 1/2 dozen rolls.

## Sugar Glaze:

2 cups sifted powdered sugar
1/4 cup hot water
1 teaspoon soft butter

Mix ingredients well and drizzle over warm bunnies.

# Shaping Bunnies:

To shape each bunny, you will need a 10" strip of dough for the body and a 5" strip for the head. The strips are made by pinching off a small amount of dough and rolling it between your hands to the desired length. As shown in the illustration below, form a loose pinwheel with the strip for the body and another, smaller, close to it for the head. The body and head will "grow" together as the dough rises. For ears, pinch off 1 1/2" strips and roll into cigar shape and place next to the head. Pinch off a bit of dough and roll into a ball for the tail.

# Roast Leg of Lamb and Potatoes

1 leg of lamb, 4 to 6 pounds
6 russet potatoes
2 onions
salt

Thinly slice potatoes and onions. Place in large bowl of salted water. Meanwhile, in shallow casserole dish, roast the lamb for 1 hour in 350° oven. Drain potatoes and onions, pat dry with paper towel. Place under and around lamb in casserole. Salt to taste. Continue cooking for another hour to hour and a half, basting with drippings from the lamb, until desired doneness and the potatoes are a crispy brown. If the lamb does not produce much liquid for basting, pour 1/4 to 1/2 cup beef broth over all. Serves 6 to 8.

*Easter Vacation, 1950*

# Lamb Terrapin for Leftover Lamb

2 cups cooked, diced lamb
2 hard-boiled eggs, chopped
2 tablespoons vegetable oil
1 tablespoon lemon juice
2 tablespoons butter
2 tablespoons flour
1 teaspoon dry mustard
2 cups lamb stock or milk
1 teaspoon Worcestershire sauce
salt, pepper
rice, cooked

Combine lamb, eggs, oil and lemon juice and set aside. Melt butter. Blend with flour and dry mustard. Slowly stir in lamb stock or milk. Add Worcestershire sauce, salt and pepper to taste. Cook until bubbly. Add lamb mixture and heat in double boiler. Serve over rice. Serves 4.

# Minted Green Peas

2 tablespoons butter or margarine
6 leaves lettuce
6 to 8 sprigs fresh mint
1/2 teaspoon salt
1 tablespoon sugar
1/4 cup water
2 packages frozen peas

Melt butter or margarine in medium saucepan. Arrange a layer of lettuce leaves in butter. Add peas which have been thawed just enough to separate. Add mint, salt, sugar and water. Cover with remaining lettuce leaves. Bring to boil. Cover pan tightly. Simmer for 5 to 10 minutes. Remove mint and, if desired, lettuce. Serves 6.

# White Cake Auntie Coleman

2 egg whites or enough to make 1/4 cup
4 tablespoons warm butter (softened but not melted)
1/2 cup milk, room temperature
1 1/2 cups flour
1 heaping teaspoon baking powder
1/2 teaspoon salt
1 cup sugar
1 teaspoon vanilla

Place egg whites, butter and milk in bowl. Sift dry ingredients and add to first mixture. Beat 4 minutes. Add vanilla. Pour into 9" x 9" pan. Bake in 350° oven until cake tester comes out clean and top is lightly browned, about 30 minutes. Ice with Broiled Brown Sugar Icing, see below.

*Decorate with colored candy-coated almonds for Easter egg effect. Do not use strong tasting candies such as jelly beans. Or decorate with white chocolate Easter bunnies available at most candy stores. Use melted white chocolate to "glue" the candy to the icing.*

### Broiled Brown Sugar Icing:

3 tablespoons butter, melted
3/4 cup brown sugar, firmly packed
2 tablespoons cream
1/2 cup chopped walnuts

Mix all ingredients and spread on cake while cake is still warm. Place under broiler until bubbly. Cool.

# Fourth of July

The Fourth of July was the official start of summer. It was also two days following my twin sister's and my birthdays. We often combined the two for a gala occasion.

Red, white and blue streamers and American flags in varying sizes adorned the house. We looked forward to evening when we could wave our sparklers, watch "snakes" coil into ash, and ignite the cones which would light up the night sky. A family crowd of all ages helped us celebrate.

Daddy made mint juleps which he served with much pride and fanfare. The night before our big celebration he pulverized fresh mint, added a bottle of bourbon and a splash of white creme de menthe, and let the heady potion steep overnight. The following day he drove to the end of the island and purchased a huge sack of crushed ice just in time to fill the tall glasses. The remaining crushed ice provided the ammunition for the traditional ice fights — where the boys would try to stuff as much ice as possible down the fronts of the girls, with the girls retaliating in kind.

The chase came to an end when dinner was announced. We sat down to Mother's famous Ham Loaf with Horseradish Sauce, and the much awaited birthday cake.

*July 4th, 1979*

# Ham Loaf with Horseradish Sauce

1 1/2 pounds ground lean ham
1 1/2 pounds ground lean pork
1 cup saltine cracker crumbs
2 eggs, beaten
1 cup milk
1/2 cup rolled oats (oatmeal)
1 medium can tomato or V-8 Juice

Mix meat, eggs, milk, crumbs and oatmeal. Bake in 350° oven for 1 hour. Drain off fat. Baste with juice and bake another 1/2 hour. Serves 10.

### Horseradish Sauce:

2 tablespoons sugar
1 egg, well beaten
2 tablespoons vinegar
salt to taste
1/2 cup bottled horseradish
1 cup whipping cream

In small pan, cook sugar, egg, vinegar and salt until thick. Cool. Whip cream until stiff and fold into above mixture, along with horseradish. Serves 5.

*Serve this with baked beans (page 84), brown bread (page 93) and coleslaw (page 76).*
*-or-*
*Serve with vegetables and a rice or hominy casserole (see pages 72 through 74).*

# String Beans

For each pound of fresh, cooked beans, brown 1/3 stick (about 3 tablespoons) of butter. Add salt and pepper and 1 teaspoon of lemon juice. Toss with beans. Sprinkle with toasted, sliced almonds.

# Cheese Stuffed Zucchini

Parboil zucchini (one entire zucchini per person) until tender crisp (*al dente*); halve lengthwise, scrape out and discard centers. Spread a layer of sour cream in cavities. Fill with shredded cheddar cheese, or a combination of cheddar and jack cheeses. Top with grated Parmesan cheese. Put under broiler until cheese is melted and bubbly.

*Cocktails on Patio,*
*Summer, 1939*

# Hominy Grits

3/4 cup hominy grits
1 teaspoon salt
2 cups boiling water
1/4 cup (1/2 stick) butter
1 tablespoon sugar
1 egg, unbeaten
2 cups milk
brown sugar

Gradually pour hominy into boiling, salted water. Add 1 cup milk. Cook one hour in double boiler, stirring occasionally. Beat egg and remaining cup of milk. Add this, along with sugar and butter, to hominy. Put into greased casserole. Cover with brown sugar. Bake in 325° oven for one hour. Serves 6.

# Mrs. Robert E. Lee's Spoonbread

1 pint milk
1/4 cup white cornmeal
1 tablespoon butter
3 eggs, well beaten
2 tablespoons flour
pinch of salt

Bring milk to a boil. Sprinkle in cornmeal and cook, stirring constantly, until mixture thickens slightly. Stir in butter. Set aside to cool, then beat in eggs, flour, and salt. Turn into greased, shallow 1 quart bake dish. Bake in 375° oven for about 35 minutes. Serve at once. Serves 4.

# Cheese Poppyseed Rice

1 cup uncooked white rice
2 cups water
1/2 teaspoon salt
1/8 teaspoon pepper
2 teaspoons prepared mustard
1 cup grated sharp cheddar cheese
1 cup milk
1 egg, beaten
1 tablespoon poppy seeds
2 tablespoons butter or margarine
1/2 teaspoon paprika

Combine water, salt and rice in 2 quart saucepan. Bring to vigorous boil. Cover and simmer 14 minutes. Remove from heat, keep lid on 10 minutes longer. Stir into hot rice the pepper, mustard, 1/2 cup cheese, milk and egg. Spread evenly in well greased shallow casserole. Sprinkle on poppy seeds and remaining cheese. Cut butter over top and sprinkle on paprika. Put under broiler until heated through and browned. Serves 6 to 8.

*Twins on Porch,*
*Summer 1937*

# Skillet Custard Cornbread

1/3 cup sifted flour
1 cup yellow cornmeal
2 teaspoons baking powder
1 teaspoon salt
2 tablespoons sugar
1 egg, well beaten
1 3/4 cup milk
1 tablespoon butter, melted

Sift flour, cornmeal, baking powder, salt and sugar. Combine egg and 1 cup milk.  Add to dry ingredients. Stir until well mixed.  Melt shortening in 9" skillet and pour in batter. Pour remaining 3/4 cup milk over batter. Do not stir. Bake in 350° oven for 25 minutes. Serves 6.

*If the skillet handle is not oven proof, cover it completely with aluminum foil before baking.*

# Nancy's Caraway Coleslaw

1 cup mayonnaise
1/2 cup chopped green onion
2 tablespoons red wine vinegar
1 tablespoon sweet pickle juice
1/2 teaspoon garlic salt
1/2 teaspoon salt
1/2 teaspoon pepper
3/4 teaspoon caraway seeds
a few drops of lemon juice
4 cups shredded cabbage

Mix first eight ingredients until well blended. Add lemon and mix. Add shredded cabbage and stir. Refrigerate several hours or overnight, stirring occasionally. Serves 6 to 8.

*For extra flavor, add chunks of pineapple, apple or mandarin oranges and toasted, slivered almonds. Garnish with slices of avocado and hard-boiled eggs.*

# Nutty Orange Cake

1/2 cup sugar
1/2 cup (1 stick) butter, softened
1/2 cup fine dry bread crumbs
1/2 cup finely chopped walnuts

Mix all ingredients together and pat firmly on bottom and part way up sides of greased 10" tube pan.

1 package white cake mix
1/2 cup orange juice
1/2 cup orange marmalade
1 cup chopped walnuts

Prepare a cake using packaged white cake mix substituting 1/2 cup orange juice as part of the liquid called for. Add orange marmalade and chopped walnuts. Mix until well blended. Pour into tube pan and bake in 350° oven for 55 minutes. Cool for 10 minutes. Remove from pan. Spread icing over cake, (see below).

### Nutty Orange Cake Icing:

2 tablespoons butter, softened
3 teaspoons orange juice, room temperature
1 cup powdered sugar

Mix with electric mixer until smooth.

*Before placing a freshly baked cake on a serving plate, sprinkle the plate with powered sugar to prevent the cake from sticking to the plate.*

# Lubelle's Thin Chocolate Sheet Cake

4 tablespoons (1/2 stick) butter, softened
1 cup brown sugar, firmly packed
1 egg, beaten
1 cup cake flour, sifted and measured three times
1/2 cup milk
1/2 cup sweetened cocoa
4 to 5 tablespoons boiling water
1 teaspoon vanilla
pinch of salt
1/2 teaspoon baking soda

Cream butter and sugar. Stir in egg and 2 tablespoons of flour. Add remaining flour alternately with milk, saving out one tablespoon of flour. Make paste of cocoa and boiling water. Add to above along with the vanilla and salt. At the very end, add the last tablespoon of flour and the soda. Mix all together with electric mixer. Pour into small rectangular pan about 7" x 10". Bake in 350° oven for 25 to 30 minutes. Cool and frost with Chocolate Glaze Frosting (see page 79).

*To make your own cake flour, add 2 tablespoons of cornstarch for each cup of flour. Sift twice and then measure.*

## Chocolate Glaze Frosting

3 squares (3 ounces) unsweetened chocolate
2 tablespoons butter
1 cup sugar
1/2 cup whipping cream
1 teaspoon vanilla
pinch of salt
chopped nuts, optional

Melt 2 squares chocolate with butter. Add sugar and cream. Bring to a rolling boil, remove from fire and add 1 square chocolate cut into small pieces. Beat gently until smooth. Add vanilla, salt and, if desired, the nuts (walnuts, pecans, almonds, macadamia or hazel). When cooled and thickened, spread over cake.

## Mock Sachertorte

Using packaged mix, prepare Devil's Food Cake and cut into two layers. Spread raspberry jam between layers. Ice with Chocolate Glaze Frosting (see above).

*Nancy's and Sally's birthday, 1977*

# Other Special Occasions

The beach house attracted a constant stream of house guests, where love and laughter embraced the air. Weekends found the extra bedrooms in the big old house brimming over with friends and family. My twin sister and I shared one room, and my brother had his own room with double bunk beds. When the guest rooms were full, the boys slept in sleeping bags on the living room floor or on the front brick patio. It wasn't at all unusual at breakfast time to find a hungry guest peering sleepily through the window.

On occasions, my brother John donned the "chef's apron" and spent an entire morning in the kitchen busily preparing his specialties of Glopped-Up Beans and Spicey Spaghetti Sauce. The aroma from the simmering pots was intoxicating.

My sister and I watched and learned while our grandmother and our Swedish "nanny," Neenie, produced mouthwatering doughnuts, breads, rolls and pies. One of our favorite treats was stirring up a pan of creamy Chocolate Fudge with Cherries, which was devoured after dinner while we sat outside in the balmy, starlit night listening to John's close friend play "Greensleeves" on his recorder. He called me his "Demon Enchantress." He was on his way to graduate school, and I was just sixteen.

Mother graciously hosted many successful bridge and bridal luncheons and numerous lunches for visiting guests. The dining room table was handsomely set with the best linen and tableware that the beach house had to offer. Festive, frothy and exotic cool drinks, which we called Pink Ladies, were served with a flair. Frozen daiquiris were dressed up with colorful paper parasols speared through maraschino cherries and slices of pineapple or orange.

Mother's recipe book was filled with a variety of hot and cold dishes which she served with homemade rolls and bread. The highlight of many luncheons was a beautiful dessert: Aunt Clara's Blitz Torte — layers of white cake and rich custard, crowned with giant red strawberries.

*Beach house dining room, "anytime"*

# John's Spicey Spaghetti Sauce

4 onions, sliced or chopped
2 tablespoons olive oil
2 pounds ground round
2 teaspoons each oregano, basil and thyme
salt, pepper
1 1/2 cups burgundy wine
1 large can tomatoes
2 small cans tomato paste
1 package spaghetti, cooked

Fry onions in oil until transparent and soft. Add ground round, break apart with fork and cook with onions until pinkish in color. Add spices and wine, tomatoes and tomato paste. Cover and simmer several hours until it cooks down and becomes thick. Serve over spaghetti. Serves 8 to 10.

*If there is too much grease in the spaghetti sauce, add a few thin slices of potato to the sauce as it cooks to absorb the excess. Remove potato slices before serving.*

# John's Glopped-up Beans

8 strips bacon, cut into pieces
4 onions, sliced
1 3/4 cups catsup
1 rounded tablespoon prepared mustard
1 teaspoon Worcestershire sauce
1/2 cup brown sugar, firmly packed
1 cup burgundy wine
salt
1/2 teaspoon nutmeg
1 teaspoon rosemary
2 large cans pork and beans
extra brown sugar (for topping)

In frying pan, cook onions and bacon together until onions are transparent and soft. Mix together the rest of the ingredients and add to above. Place in casserole, cover, and bake in 250° oven for about 5 hours. Sprinkle liberally with extra brown sugar, which will form a crust as beans continue to bake. Bake for an additional hour uncovered. Serves 12.

*Serve with Nancy's Caraway Coleslaw (page 76) and Little Brown Breads (page 93).*

# John's Pizza

### Crust:

2 1/3 cups sifted flour
1 tablespoon Crisco
1/4 teaspoon salt
1/4 teaspoon pepper
1 package yeast
2/3 cup warm water
olive oil
2 small cans tomato sauce
tomato paste

Sprinkle yeast in water. Mix first four ingredients. Add dissolved yeast and knead until smooth and elastic, about 5 minutes. Let rise until double in size. Halve the dough. Roll into thin circle or square and place on ungreased cookie sheet or pizza pan. Pinch and curl up edges to hold topping. Oil dough with olive oil. Thicken 2 small cans tomato sauce with a little tomato paste and spread over dough to cover. Add topping.

### Topping:

oregano
strips of good quality salami
chopped green or white onions
mushrooms and anchovies, (both optional)
grated Provoloni or mild cheddar cheese
grated Parmesan cheese
garlic salt
olive oil

Sprinkle crust generously with oregano. Place strips of salami on top. Add chopped onions, mushrooms, anchovies and grated Provoloni or cheddar cheese. Sprinkle with Parmesan cheese. Mix garlic salt in olive oil and drizzle over pizza. Bake in 400° oven for 15 to 20 minutes or until edges turn crispy brown and cheese has melted. Makes 2 large pizzas.

# Mildred's Beef Casserole

1 onion, chopped
1 tablespoon vegetable oil
1 pound ground round
1 packet George Washington Seasoning and Broth Powder
1 cup cold water
1 cup cheddar cheese, grated
1 8 oz. package of noodles
1 or 2 cans cream of mushroom soup
buttered bread crumbs

Brown onions slightly. Add meat and cook until meat looses its pink color. Dissolve broth powder in cold water. Add to meat and simmer for 10 minutes. Cook noodles and add along with cheese. Put in buttered casserole. Pour soup over above. Top with bread crumbs. Bake in 350° oven for 35 to 45 minutes. Serves 6.

# Chocolate Fudge with Cherries

2 squares (2 ounces) unsweetened chocolate, cut into pieces
2 cups sugar
1/8 teaspoon salt
3/4 cup cream
2 tablespoons light corn syrup
2 tablespoons butter
1 teaspoon vanilla
1/3 cup chopped nuts (walnuts, pecans, macadamia)
1/3 cup diced maraschino cherries

Combine first five ingredients. Stir over quick heat until sugar dissolves. Cook slowly, stirring frequently, until the soft ball stage on your candy thermometer is reached, or 240°. Remove from fire and add butter. Cool slightly. Beat until begins to thicken. Stir in vanilla, chopped nuts and maraschino cherries. Pour into 8" square pan and chill until set.

# Neenie's Doughnuts

1 cup sugar
1 tablespoon butter, softened
1/4 teaspoon salt
1/4 teaspoon nutmeg
2 eggs, unbeaten
1 cup buttermilk
1 level teaspoon baking soda
1/2 teaspoon baking powder
4 cups flour
1 large (3 pounds) can Crisco
granulated or powered sugar

Mix sugar, butter and salt. Add nutmeg and eggs. Mix well. Add buttermilk and baking soda, and beat well. Mix flour and baking powder and add to above mixture. Mix well. On floured board, roll out dough and cut with doughnut cutter or two biscuit cutters, one larger than the other. The dough will be soft, so handle it gingerly. While dough rests, scoop out Crisco from can and place in large (at least 3 quarts) kettle and bring to boil. When Crisco is very hot, about 370°, drop doughnuts and doughnut holes into hot grease, a few at a time, and fry until they bubble to the top and are a golden brown. Drain on paper towels. When cool, sprinkle with granulated or powdered sugar. Makes about 3 dozen doughnuts and doughnut holes.

*To keep the Crisco clean and clear for next use, drop a few thin slices of raw potato into the boiling fat. You will also have instant potato chips.*

*Always wait until Crisco has cooled before returning it to the can.*

# Aunt Virginia's Pink Ladies

4 ounces light rum
1 pint orange sherbet
-or-
8 ounces light rum
3 pints orange sherbet

Mix in blender.  Pour into stemmed glasses from a punch bowl.

# Daiquiris

juice from 16 limes
4 cups light rum
-or-
1 small can frozen limeade or lemonade, thawed
2 limeade or lemonade cans of water
2 1/2 limeade or lemonade cans of light rum

Mix well and serve chilled in punch bowl or over crushed ice in stemmed glasses. Makes about 2 quarts or 16 to 20 drinks.

*Decorate glasses with paper parasols speared through maraschino cherries and slices of pineapple or orange.*

*Place small edible flowers, such as nasturtiums, violas or small pansies, in an ice cube tray, fill with water and freeze. Place the frozen flower ice cubes in the punch bowl.*

*- or -*

*Thinly slice oranges, lemons and limes and float them in the punch bowl.*

# Molded Fish Salad

2 tablespoons plain gelatin
1/2 cup cold water
1 1/2 cups hot water
4 tablespoons lemon juice
2 teaspoons prepared mustard
1/2 teaspoon salt
1/2 teaspoon paprika
pimiento-stuffed olives, sliced
2 cans (7 ounces each) white tuna
- or -
1 1/2 pounds cooked swordfish
2 cups chopped celery
1 cup mayonnaise

Soften gelatin in cold water, then dissolve in hot water. Mix in lemon juice, mustard, salt and paprika. Pour small amount just to cover the bottom of ring mold or fish mold. Space olives decoratively in mixture. Chill until set. Also chill the rest of the gelatin mixture until partially set or slightly thickened, then add fish, celery and mayonnaise. Add to mold and chill until set. Serve with Cucumber Dressing, (see page 90). Serves 8.

*Serve this Molded Fish Salad with deviled eggs. Garnish with edible flowers such as nasturtiums, violas or small pansies.*
*- or -*
*Cut notches in thinly sliced carrots to form flower shapes, using tiny sprigs of parsley or cilantro for the leaf.*

# Cucumber Dressing

1 cup mayonnaise
2 teaspoons tarragon or wine vinegar
1/2 teaspoon salt
dash of pepper
1/2 cup finely diced cucumber, seeds removed

Combine first four ingredients. Mix well. Stir in diced cucumber. Serve with Molded Fish Salad, (see page 89). Serves 8.

# Tomato and Cream Cheese Aspic

2 small cans tomato sauce
1 tablespoon vinegar
pinch of salt
1 box (3 ounces) lemon jello
1 avocado, cut into chunks

Mix tomato sauce, vinegar and salt. Heat and pour over lemon jello. Stir until dissolved. Add avocado and pour into 6 to 8 cup mold. Refrigerate until partially set.

### Second layer:

2 packages (3 ounces each) cream cheese, softened
1/2 cup mayonnaise
pinch of salt
1 1/2 cups boiling water
1 box (3 ounces) lemon jello

Mix cream cheese with mayonnaise and salt. Pour boiling water over jello and stir until dissolved. Refrigerate until partially set. Add to cheese mixture and pour on top of tomato aspic. Chill until firm. Serves 6 to 8.

# Bing Cherry Mold

3 boxes (3 ounces each) cherry jello
3 cans Bing cherries, drained (save juice)
2 1/4 cups sherry wine
1/2 to 3/4 cup slivered almonds

Dissolve jello in 3 cups boiling cherry juice saved from cans, or juice from cans plus enough water to make 3 cups. Stir until dissolved. Add sherry, drained cherries and almonds. Pour into 2 large ring molds. Chill until firm.

### Top with:

3 packages (8 ounces each) cream cheese, softened
1 1/2 cups mayonnaise
3 boxes (3 ounces each) lemon jello
4 1/2 cups boiling water

Mix cream cheese and mayonnaise and set aside. Pour boiling water over jello. Stir until dissolved and refrigerate until just beginning to gel and then add to cream cheese mixture, dividing evenly between the two cherry molds. Chill until set. Serves 24.

*On the beach, Summer 1937*

# Deviled Egg and Shrimp Casserole

8 eggs, hard-boiled, shelled and cooled
1/2 teaspoon salt
1/2 teaspoon dry mustard
1/4 cup mayonnaise
1 1/2 tablespoons light cream
1/2 teaspoon lemon juice
1 pound shrimp
dash of salt
1 bay leaf
2 to 3 slices of lemon
4 cups white sauce
1/2 cup grated cheddar or Swiss cheese
1 cup bread crumbs
2 tablespoons butter

Cut eggs in half, lengthwise. Put yolks through sieve or give them a whirl in the cuisinart. Season with salt. Add mustard, mayonnaise, cream and lemon juice. Fill whites with mixture. Place in shallow bake dish. If using uncooked shrimp, cook for 10 minutes in boiling water with salt, bay leaf and slices of lemon. Drain and devein. Add to bake dish, distributing evenly around eggs. Add cheese to white sauce. Pour over eggs and shrimp. Sauté bread crumbs in butter and sprinkle over top of casserole. Bake in 350° oven for 30 to 45 minutes, or until bubbly. Serves 6.

*This dish is hearty enough for a Friday night dinner!*

# Grape-Nuts Bread

1 cup Grape-Nuts cereal
2 cups buttermilk
1 teaspoon baking soda
1 cup sugar
1 egg, beaten
2 tablespoons butter, melted
3 1/2 cups flour
4 teaspoons baking powder
1 teaspoon salt

Soak Grape-Nuts in buttermilk and baking soda for 15 minutes. Add remaining ingredients. Pour into greased bread pan. Let stand for 20 minutes. Bake in 350° oven for about 45 minutes or until cake tester comes out clean. Makes 1 loaf.

# Little Brown Breads

1 cup yellow cornmeal
1/2 cup flour
1/2 teaspoon salt
1 teaspoon baking powder
1 teaspoon baking soda
1/2 cup graham flour (found in health food stores)
6 tablespoons molasses
1 egg, beaten
1/4 cup vegetable oil
1 cup buttermilk
1/2 cup raisins or currants
1/2 cup chopped walnuts

Sift cornmeal, flour, salt, baking powder and baking soda. Stir in graham flour. Combine molasses, egg, oil and buttermilk. Beat into dry mixture until smooth. Stir in raisins and nuts. Fill greased muffin cups 2/3 full. Bake in 425° oven for 20 minutes. Makes 12 muffins.

# Orange Yeast Bread

1 large orange
1/4 cup sugar
1/4 cup hot water
1 teaspoon salt
3 tablespoons Crisco
1 package yeast
2 tablespoons lukewarm water
1 teaspoon sugar
1 egg, slightly beaten
4 to 4 1/2 cups flour

Halve orange, remove white center and grind very fine in blender or food processor. Add 1/4 cup sugar, hot water, salt and Crisco. Heat in saucepan over medium flame until it comes to a boil. Cool to lukewarm. Dissolve yeast in lukewarm water, add 1 teaspoon sugar and stir into lukewarm orange mixture. Add beaten egg, and as much flour as needed to make a soft dough. Toss on lightly floured board and knead until elastic and non-sticky. Place in greased 9" x 5" loaf pan. Cover and let rise until nearly double. Bake in 350° oven for 45 to 55 minutes. Makes 1 loaf.

*Volleyball on the Sand, Summer 1938*

# Raised Muffins

1 pint milk, scalded
1/4 cup (1/2 stick) butter, softened
1/4 cup sugar
1 teaspoon salt
1 package yeast
4 cups flour
2 eggs, beaten

Put sugar, butter and salt into bowl. Scald milk and pour over. When lukewarm, dissolve yeast in mixture. Add 2 level cups flour and let stand in warm place until light and "full of bubbles." Stir in eggs and 2 more cups flour. Let rise until double, about 20 minutes. Punch down with floured spoon. Grease muffin tins and fill half full. Let rise until double. Bake in 400° oven for 5 minutes; then in 350° oven for 15 minutes more. Makes about 1 1/2 dozen large muffins.

# Baked Prune Whip

3 egg whites, beaten stiff
scant 1/2 cup sugar
1 tablespoon lemon juice
pinch of salt
1 cup cooked prune purée (about 20 cooked, pitted prunes)

Purée prunes. Beat egg whites and fold in sugar, prunes and lemon juice. Place into 1 quart bake dish in pan of hot water in 325° oven for about 1 hour. Serve with Custard Sauce. Serves 4 to 6.

### Custard Sauce:

Combine 3 egg yolks, beaten, with 2 cups milk, 3 tablespoons sugar and 1/2 teaspoon vanilla. Heat at low heat until thickened.

# Blitz Torte Auntie Clara

1/4 cup (1/2 stick) butter
1/2 cup sugar
4 egg yolks, beaten
1 cup flour
4 teaspoons baking powder
pinch of salt
1/4 cup milk
1 teaspoon vanilla
4 egg whites, beaten stiff
3/4 cups sugar
1/3 cup slivered almonds

Cream together butter and sugar. Add beaten egg yolks. Mix flour, baking powder and salt. Add to creamed mixture alternately with milk. Add vanilla. Spread in 2 shallow cake pans. Mix beaten egg whites with 3/4 cup sugar. Divide evenly, spread over batter and sprinkle with almonds. Bake in 325° oven for 30 minutes. Cool.

### Filling:

1 tablespoon cornstarch
1/4 cup sugar
2 egg yolks, slightly beaten
1 cup milk, scalded
whipping cream (for topping)
whole strawberries

In top of double boiler, mix cornstarch and sugar. Add beaten egg yolks. Scald milk and pour over the mixture. Cook, stirring constantly, until thick. Spread between cooled cake layers. Cover top of cake with sweetened whipped cream and whole strawberries. Serves 8.

# Nancy's French Chocolate Cake

8 tablespoons (1 stick) butter, softened
1 bag of almonds (6 ounces),
- or -
1 cup of filberts with skin on
1/4 cup very fine bread crumbs
3/4 cup chocolate chips,
- or -
4 squares (4 ounces) semi-sweet chocolate
2/3 cup sugar
3 eggs, unbeaten
1 tablespoon dark rum or cognac
pinch of salt

Using about 1 1/2 tablespoons of butter from above, thoroughly grease the bottom and sides of an 8" round springform cake pan. Line the bottom with wax paper cut to fit, buttering it generously. Grind nuts as fine as possible.

Melt chocolate over simmering, not boiling, water. Cream remaining butter with electric beater until soft and light. Gradually work in sugar until mixture is very light and fluffy. When all sugar is added, add eggs, one at a time, beating hard after each addition. The mixture will look curdled, but that's all right. Stir in melted chocolate, nuts, bread crumbs, rum or cognac, and salt. Mix well and pour into pan. Bake at 375° for 25 minutes. Remove from oven and allow to cool on rack. Turn out onto plate. Cover with Chocolate Cake Glaze (see page 98).

*This cake can also be served with Creme Anglaise (page 99) spooned around individual portions.*

### Chocolate Cake Glaze:

2 squares (2 ounces) unsweetened chocolate
1 square (1 ounce) semi-sweet chocolate
2 teaspoons honey
4 tablespoons (1/2 stick) butter, softened and cut into pieces
toasted almonds or filberts, optional

Melt the chocolates over hot, not boiling, water. Stir in honey and butter. Mix well. Cool until it is somewhat thickened, then pour over top of cake, smoothing it down the sides with a spatula. Garnish with nuts, if desired. Serves 6 to 8.

*For special occasions, decorate this rich cake with tiny white chocolate hearts, bells, shells or other shapes. Simply melt the chocolate and, with a small spoon, carefully spoon it into molds and freeze until set. Use more melted chocolate to "glue" the shapes to the cake.*

# Creme Anglaise

1 cup milk, scalded
1/2 vanilla bean, split lengthwise
3 egg yolks
1/4 cup sugar

Scald milk with vanilla bean. Whisk the egg yolks and sugar in top of double boiler off the heat until lemon color. Warm mixture over simmering water, stirring continuously. Slowly pour in scalded milk and vanilla bean and continue to stir until the mixture slightly thickens, or for about 20 minutes. Strain. Cool, stirring from time to time. Refrigerate.

*Daddy in "Gemini," Albatros 8*
*Summer 1942*

# To End...

The memories of family and good times past, which are intertwined with the recipes presented in this book, are also totally engulfed with memories of the old family beach house which, regrettably, is no more.

The following poem by James S. Hamilton so captures the nostalgia of my memories that I have saved it for many years, and now I wish to share it with you, hopeful that it will rekindle your own special memories.

## THIS OLD HOUSE
*by James S. Hamilton*

*It isn't years that make us call it old,*
    *Nor creaking stairs, nor rattling windowpanes,*
*Nor little rifts that smuggle in the cold,*
    *Nor a patch of roof that dribbles when it rains.*
*For old is only what affection calls*
    *All its familiar, best-remembered things —*
*The roof of home, the kindly sheltering walls,*
    *To which in memory it always clings.*

*It never could be really old, this place*
　　　*Where never anything but youth has been.*
*In every corner lingers some young face*
　　　*That time can never quench the laughter in.*
*Locked in the walls are echoes of young joys,*
　　　*Of song and shouts and spirits high and free.*
*The rooms are thronging with the ghosts of boys*
　　　*The happy, happy boys we used to be.*

*If we believe that nothing ever dies,*
　　　*That nothing ever passes quite away,*
*It cannot be but something hidden lies*
　　　*Here in this house, beyond the sight of day.*
*There must go somewhere, all those bits of us*
　　　*We leave behind when we grow into men —*
*The hopes and dreams so multitudinous*
　　　*We somehow lose and never find again.*

*Here is their home, where brotherhood began,*
　　　*And friendship learned its beauty and its power,*
*Here where the boy began to be a man,*
　　　*And life first showed beyond the present hour.*
*So all the things we dreamed and did not do —*
　　　*The songs within us that were never sung,*
*Stay on forever fresh and ever new,*
　　　*Stay on and on, to keep this old house young.*

*And though the house may go, they linger yet,*
　　　*For youth is in them and they cannot die.*
*And we may go, but never quite forget.*
　　　*Some day a breeze is sure to wander by,*
*Soft with the spring-smell of our younger years*
　　　*Or scent of smoke out of some autumn wood,*
*To tell us, though the telling brings us tears,*
　　　*Youth is still here — here where the old house stood.*

*Beach House, 1949*

# Index